A Mask Best Worn 'Til Midnight

Chezney Martin

BookLeaf Publishing

Presentation by *BookLeaf Publishing*

Web: www.bookleafpub.com

E-mail: info@bookleafpub.com

ISBN: 978-93-95755-48-1

First edition 2022

ACKNOWLEDGEMENT

For my parents and sister, and loving partner Barry; without whom, there are many things I would not have done nor do. Heidi, my rez-dog, is an honourable mention for her constant, persistent, not-taking-no-for-an-answer emotional support.

For readers; I hope you find comfort and strength, any at all, in my words, because these poems are for you, too.

PREFACE

It became an aspiration of mine to publish a collection of poetry when I was nine years old. In 2007, my first poem was a rhyming couplet sequence that won first place in the small, but mighty, Community Awareness Week Poetry Contest held in my home community of Six Nations.

Poetry became, and permanently remains, an old friend that aids me in processing difficult emotions, thoughts and reactions. It is the open document on my laptop, the notepad resting underneath a pen on my dresser, and the sticky note stuck to my calendar.

I wanted the publishing process for this anthology to be a rewarding challenge. I wanted it to be freeing, and serve as a means of sharing the bandages that helped me heal old wounds. Of course, certain topics aren't always pleasant: I wanted this work to be carried by a publisher that understood it as a form of medicine.

I am now sincerely daunted and delighted to share this as a true and raw piece of myself. The title comes from the mask I wear, whether I am in front of family, friends, colleagues or online, and it is the acknowledgement of the freedom in taking the mask off at night, at home, in safety, where I can be myself.

I hope that if readers take something, anything, away from this work, it's that Indigenous women are so much more than the obstacles that force us to define who we are, and the stereotypes attached to us that often speak before we do.

With kindness,

Chezney Martin

Borrowing

The smell of sunset and sweetness
mingled with roadside dust and the sound of
passing cars
We pulled over, together
scissors in hand and a shared calm
We picked just enough of the blade
so it would grow back
like the old ones used to do
before we walked this earth

Spirit

I am spiritual
but not religious

I will not retrieve food that has fallen from my
plate
slipped out of my hands
so that my visitors can eat
I have enough to share

I will not whistle into the darkness of night
or sing songs I don't know the meaning ofSo I
don't call things to me
things I shouldn't see anyway

I will not walk where a snake has crossed
in front of me or behind
so I don't find what is to be left in hiding
I can respect secrecy

I will not shake hands with strangers
at gatherings or in ceremony
so I don't take something with me
something that shouldn't be offered in the first
place

I will speak to my ancestors
tell them stories of my life and woes
so that they know
I know they're there

But I cannot believe in rules
that predict what will happen when I die
none of us have died to know
I will live my life governed by nature

I can respect the world and its laws
and hold reverence and superstition to things I
cannot see
but I will not live my life
according to passages made by man

It is woman that danced this continent into being
therefore I am divine in what I choose to live by
I refuse to stay in line with the words of men
the very same that were given life by women

I am spiritual
but not religious

Home

I always go against the grain
for I can't care much about a society
that was not made for me
I need one with warmth, at least

Warmth and love
eyes that see fatigue and sadness
and offer remedies of sleep and laughter
That is what I need

I know there used to be a place
one that doesn't exist anymore
and I know I sit amongst thousands
who yearn for that same place

Maybe one day,
we can build it
If not for us,
then for our children

Power

In a room full of eyes
I feel my chest tighten
Words turn into a road
one I cannot follow

Expectations are tight
tension wound snug in the air
If I can't catch my breath
how will I speak?

But this room is not mine
and I must make it so
When most uncomfortable
I remember who I am

So call forth the storm clouds
let my grandfathers listen
For when I speak and let loose thunder
the ground will shake

Measurements

By your standards
I am too loud
too strong
too big
too outspoken
too much

My waistline isn't where it should be
My hair isn't the right colour
My face isn't slim
My nose isn't pointed

I don't listen enough
sit down enough
cook enough
be kind enough
be enough

But,
My body is borrowed
derived from those that came before

They rejoice in the afterlife when I eat
where they would have went hungry
They applaud when I speak

where they would have been silent
They laugh when I go my own way
where their paths were already laid

By our standards
I am being what must be

Education

I haven't spoken yet, nor shared my ideas
Already I am painted black, a shadow
an undesigned avatar
because to them, I don't belong

Ingenuity, innovation can come from anywhere
But the quietness of my composure
must mean I have none
Right?

Hours from home
no comforts, the same I took for granted in sight
But I am expected to be functional, normal
in a space I am not welcome

They don't know how uncomfortable it is
for someone like me
But they deem my discomfort as a sign of truth
etched into the stigmas attached to my skin

Little do they know
my people mapped the stars, the land
they knew this world like the dimples in their
skin
They were engineers, inventors, scientists, too

Their thoughts are told in the stories, sung in the
songs
Their gratitude is in ceremony, spoken in our
tongues
So how can I not be among them in this life,
when their brilliance carved who I am?

Institutions will make rules for defining
intelligence
and miss out on knowing mine

Resignation

The goals can be important
they can lift up the spirit
they can help us shine in working as one
But sometimes they aren't carried with love

Taking a "break"
can feel like more work
getting ready for another round
a round that shouldn't be scheduled

Sometimes a break doesn't rejuvenate
It doesn't reenergize
It doesn't motivate
It doesn't repurpose

When and if you step away
and come back still exhausted
I know it now as a letter from the body
writing "this isn't the place for you"

And sometimes
that feeling of guilt, remorse
will creep in, seep in like poison
Yet it is us that need the antidote

Our bodies aren't made for environments
that need time to recollect lost vision

Lateral

Not all spaces are safe
Not all people are safe
But accountability can grow few and far
between
nonexistent if we're honest

Frustration manifests in many situations
just like water can be ice, snow and fog
A ladder upon which spite trickles down
instead of lifting up the feet of those climbing it

I wish you knew that attacking my personhood,
my performance
because you are lacking, or you feel lacking
tells more about who you are
than it does me

So I don't want to take your seeds
and pack them away into a place where they'll
grow
What you're trying to give isn't welcome
it's parasitic

Let it eat you alive
because I refuse

Mend

12

I used to ask
'Why is it when a certain woman,
sees another woman jovial, lively,
she comes to silence her?'
for I used to be silenced
But I know the answer—
it's because she needs to heal

Apathy

I shared a story with you
with tears in my eyes
looking, searching to be soothed
but you looked through me

You saw me as someone deceitful
not someone needing support
or words of comfort
but someone seeking attention

"You're so lucky," you say
"Only pretty girls have stalkers"
and those words burned into my eyelids
so when I closed my eyes, I still saw them

I wanted to rip my skin off
peel off the 'pretty' you called out
climb out of the skin of the shell
that you painted as to be blamed

Sometimes I wish I could take it off
everything that makes me a woman, like dirty
overalls
so that I could live and walk and breathe in
peace

To this day, I can't laugh in peace

Is it really my fault
or is it the fault of a world that doesn't protect
the most vulnerable and precious
because our world is still reeling from damage

But I will never forget your face, a woman
yourself
how quickly you said those words to me
and didn't even realize
that you were making me bleed

Mask

I prefer not to wear it all of the time
but when I don't
I become a walking irritant
invisible to those around me

I can feel it the same as fire licking my skin
It follows like a shadow, waiting
Hiding in the eyes of those that would rather not
see me bare faced, 'unkempt' they call it

Though it is the stature I wake to everyday
I have the face of my mother
The eyes of my father
I share the nose of my grandfather with my sister

Yet I am still viewed with disdain
by those that would rather not get beyond my
appearance
the very same that would be curt instead of kind
Doors are never opened for me, but closed

But if I give time to it
the mask, of course
I am met with kindness
I am visible once more

Friends are bountiful
drinks appear in my open hands
comments and niceties are free
greetings are made with smiles and winks

It is night and day
the worst of sentiments
But I can count on ten fingers
how many times I wished to be bare

When a man had over stepped, come too close
too quickly
Or when a hand touched me where I did not
want
I could fly home and take it all off
My bareness a protector, a warder of evil

So if you ask me why I wear it
I will tell you the truth
it is because sometimes
I want to be seen

Apology

If I could wash away the bruises
I would sit and lather you everyday
If I could remove the words that cut you
I would rewind time and mute them

But I can't remove the hurts
I can't wash them away or rewind them
they are yours to bear the weight of
but I can be a pillar

I can carry some of the weight
to help you stay on course and on time
because your hurt is my own
and I am here with you

If I could cast a spell
to keep you out of harms way
and far from the evil in others
I would cast it a thousand times

Just to be sure you would be safe
because you deserve peace
not bruises, cuts and breaks
by his hands

Decade

If I could sit down with myself
when she was ten
I would sit with her
an owl perched before an owlet

I would smile knowingly
and lift her chin with my hand
Her eyes mirrors of mine
Her expression known but unknown at once

I would tell her 'it will be okay
it might seem like it won't be
But it will be
Give it time'

'Your mistakes aren't worth harming yourself
cutting into your flesh and digging in
You have a right to learn and a right to act
the shame you hold is inherited'

'Let yourself be human
and allow yourself to experience
avert your gaze from those that will stifle you
They have their own healing to do'

'Who you are cannot be measured by those
around you
that measurement is yours alone'
I would hold her tight and dust her off
and tell her to go after the world

Cheese

I eat alone
on more nights than not
Prying eyes and mouths full of judgement
aren't my cup of tea

I seek solace in flavour
an embrace that is unique to no one
It is made to be eaten
and so, it won't complain

It won't ask if I did ten pushups
Or achieved a step count goal
It won't look me up and down
and say 'time to go to the gym'

I can be without a worry in the world
and have it take me on a trip
to Venice, Spain or Italy in one bite
So forgive my indulgence

There was a time I would go without
I would avoid and pretend I didn't need it
I would go to sleep instead of eating supper
and that empty pang in my stomach drove me
mad

But at least I looked skinny
with a handful of fallen hair in my hand
standing in the shower
pale and gaunt, at least I looked skinny

So forgive me for healing, for finding myself in
food
because there was a time I didn't eat
There was a time I was the judge
that told me I couldn't be loved

And let's face it
golden lava encompassing a hand spun pillow
a warm hug over the tongue after a long day
beats being hungry

Delusion

'Why won't you believe what I say,
instead of what you see?'
is the extent of a deluded tongue
whispering sweet nothings to a corpse

It's an invitation
a guide into an empty shack
under the premise that it is a mansion
shining with extravagance

True words can be spun
as people can be delusions, too
We can place them on a shelf
unreachable by others, even ourselves

And unfortunately, that isn't their fantasy
but our own

Lesson

A night of wine and dancing
sweaty hands and frizzy hair
friendly laughter and jokes abound
a group of us in a club as if no one else was
there

Ending the night on the curb-side
deciding where we would ride home
I chose a vehicle driven by someone
I didn't know

The highway was near
And the fog cleared from my eyes
I could feel the blood drain from my face
as I watched the streetlights become lines

Laughter and stupor continued
while my heart pounded in my ears
The speedometer rung true
140 and weaving through vehicles at midnight

I could have kicked myself
how stupid I was to have gotten inside
If I was to be taught a lesson in that moment
it was a lesson deserved

I couldn't forget
it was a week after the accident
one that took a loved one
and held her tight on her journey in spirit

So many things could have changed in seconds
a late brake or a missed steer
I wept
and never did it again

Severed

We used to laugh
unparalleled by anything else
We could be ourselves
shared experiences made it meaningful

But every good thing comes to an end
I think that's what they say
Where trust used to be
there was hollowness

Maybe we outgrew each other
or grew a part like a split road
Something solidified an impasse
one neither of us wanted to cross

Your home was mine and mine yours
but the doors were closed and empty
as if we had never met
nor shared such amity

And I can tell you from my soul
that I miss everything we shared
The time, the laughs, the experiences
I wish I was more mature, intuitive

If I had the foresight to know something was
special
I could have scrapped my pride
in favour of salvaging something worthwhile
with you, a person I don't know anymore

Rescue

Dear little person living on my floor
You don't do much for anyone
You can't sweep nor tidy rooms
You can't hang clothes nor wash dishes

But here you remain
a friendly alarm to the inner clock you have
You make demands with no will to enforce them
and I will concede because you fill empty spaces

When someone we love leaves
we miss them together
And somedays I wouldn't get out of bed if not
for you
I wouldn't go outside if not for you

Laughter is a gift you give when you can
you can lift me up without words
I wouldn't have thought of you in this way
When I first saw you on the staircase outside

I didn't pick you
You picked me

Shade

You knew me better than me
because I showed you everything
There were no hiding spots
we didn't know together

You could talk for me because you knew what I
would say
I'd mention a gift and it would show up in my
hands under your grin
One look and we could burst into laughter
but summer becomes winter, eventually

Anything that you couldn't do, I would do for
you
Anything I couldn't do, you would do for you
I wanted to pretend I didn't see it
matted hair kept hidden by an elaborate up-do

You wore a different face in front of me than
everyone else
I thought it was our closeness and understanding
But when I shone, you would bring in the shade
As if clouds were easy to come by

Two stars can shine at once but you wanted
novelty
Nothing that made us equals was enough
You should have known better
I should have, too

I still offered wood from my pile to feed your
fire
and you let it burn me
From where you took sadness away
you put sadness back

Even though you were half of me and I half of
you
there are pieces of me that didn't follow
I had to say good bye
because I knew you better than you did

Illness

My dearest friend,
you filled rooms with laughter
you were the cheeky and mouthy one
you were the one that brought things to life
But you wore a hat that read 'depression'
and still
nobody knew

I wish I could write to you
to tell you the truth
I have now been to more funerals
than weddings
and I miss you

Partner

If I begin my journey before you
I'll stay behind to help you
from the other side
So you can reach the heights we dreamed of

But if you begin your journey before me
they'll have to make enough room for two
so I can lie there
beside you